The
ROAD HOME

A TRUE STORY

JAY TEMBO

WestBow Press books may be ordered through booksellers or by contacting:

WestBow Press
A Division of Thomas Nelson & Zondervan
1663 Liberty Drive
Bloomington, IN 47403
www.westbowpress.com
1 (844) 714-3454

ISBN: 978-1-6642-0866-7 (sc)
ISBN: 978-1-6642-0865-0 (e)

Library of Congress Control Number: 2020920068

Print information available on the last page.

WestBow Press rev. date: 10/20/2020

WESTBOW
PRESS®
A DIVISION OF THOMAS NELSON
& ZONDERVAN

The ROAD HOME

My paternal grandfather was from Mozambique. He was a small, round-faced man with a passion to accumulate wealth. My grandmother, small like her husband, generated ambition in her children. My grandfather made a meager living from raising cattle and farming.

My father was born in a small town called Chinhoyi. My father moved to Kwekwe when he was twenty-two years old and opened a grocery store in a busy neighborhood. The store prospered, and he called his uncle to help him. His uncle eventually took charge of the business. After a couple of more years, he brought in his first cousins to help run the business but decided to close due to mismanagement by his cousins. He decided to move to Zambia in 1974, and 1979 was the year I was born.

We moved back to Zimbabwe in 1984 as a family. We had come through a lot together. I today feel that the relationships that are hardest to resolve are those in which we continue to long for something. As a boy, I remember enjoying watching famous TV shows, such as *Knight Rider* and *The A-Team*. I sure have vivid memories of the music video for "Thriller" by Michael Jackson. I also remember some of the unpainful memories of buying cookies and riding planes with my dad.

I am particularly fascinated by the fact that the older I grew, the more I felt like the same person I was when I was a younger.

When I was six years old, I moved with my brother, father and mum to live with my uncle in Harare. Just shortly after that, my father went to work in the United Kingdom. I expressed interest in living with him, but at that time, my mother had made plans that my brother and I should go and live with our maternal grandparents in Kwekwe. When I was seven years old, I started elementary school and was enrolled in the first grade. I was an exceptional student and excelled, graduating at the top of the class in my first, second, and third school years.

When I was nine years old, my mother decided that I should be transferred from the public school to a private Christian school, where I excelled academically and was excessively concerned with intellectual matters. I participated in extracurricular activities, such as baseball and soccer, and even became a Boy Scout. I enjoyed gardening and volunteered to grow crops, helping with various jobs such as preparing beds, planting, working on equipment, weeding, and harvesting for the school garden.

As an elementary school student, I played soccer on the school team and was famed for my rickety legs and dribbling wizardry. I didn't have to be technical to be good at it.

My maternal grandparents owned a small motel. An exciting chapter of my life as a youngster was when I worked for them as a pot scrubber and swept and mopped floors.

My parents kept copies of old bills and receipts, which have provided valuable insight and perspective considering the role of money in our history. One of my uncles was a career soldier who told me that in his experience, he had to spend months of uninterrupted training in the jungles being attacked by malaria-carrying mosquitoes where sickness was ever present and food and medical supplies were in short supply. He also shared with me the fact that occasional wine had become his sustenance and pleasure as he moved from one crisis to another.

When I was thirteen years old, my maternal grandmother passed away. As one of her youngest grandsons, I had a special affection for her. There seemed to be a natural bond between us a little outside the mainstream rush. Her funeral was among the well-to-do and required many expenses. Gloves were made for bearers and food for the guests. People were called to the funeral by word of mouth.

I remember my grandmother accusing me of straining compulsively toward impossible goals and measuring my self-worth entirely in terms of my achievements. I had not been used to doing many things other than studying. My books were my friends in all grades. I graduated top of the class.

When I was fourteen years old, my fellow eighth graders had started dating. One girl caught my attention,her name was Patience. Wow! This young lady was gorgeous and exhibited good manners. She would come to school always well dressed. Nothing about her hair, her eyes, her height, or her weight made her unattractive. I never proposed to her, but I always thought about her and that I would marry her. We would have a happy family and share our common hobbies and interests. Her communicable grin, warm disposition, cynical humor, and receiving of people with great candidness were observed by all who had the privilege to meet her. She packed several lifetimes of interests and activities, including worldwide travel, music, science, and gourmet cooking.

As I progressed into high school, I played basketball on the high school team and dictated the tempo, intensity, and rhythm of the game. At age fifteen, with God-given natural abilities of strength, speed, modesty, and exemplary character, I cared about the team by being selfless and not concerned about anything more. I encouraged my teammates to do the little things well and serve others well, and they would be blessed. I was named team vice captain. I could dribble past giant point guard opponents and easily make layups.

I was talented both at academic examinations and sports, which made my family very proud of me.

As I was approaching sixteen years of age, I was getting ready to complete high school. At age seventeen, I completed high school and returned to Zambia, where my parents were. My father wanted me to go to the university to study internal medicine. I had to choose between accounting and medical science and chose accounting because it would take a shorter period to complete. My mother and I worked hard to get me registered as a British student. I was going to become a chartered and certified accountant. I borrowed some money from my aunt in Zambia and bought some clothes. I traveled to nearby rural areas of Lusaka and exchanged some clothes for village chickens and goats. I hired a company that specialized in animal husbandry, and it took responsibility of transporting the animals to the city of Lusaka for resale. I made huge profits, which allowed me to purchase British pounds to pay for my student registration fees.

I began school in January 1998 and took the first ACCA technician examination in June. I graduated second of all students. Although my father was happy to hear about my exam success as a student, he told me that he believed the money I was paying for tuition and exam fees should have been invested in a business venture. I received a scholarship from the government of Norway to pay 50 percent of my fees for the second stage of my ACCA technician exams. I opened a shop that sold groceries—mainly confectionery products—and advertised mostly by word of mouth. The business venture was successful, and I was able to save money for my ACCA technician stage 2. I bought equipment that allowed me to study online, which included books, stationery, devices, and other learning essentials, such as breakthrough videos, standardized cassette tapes, revision kits, manuals, and videoconferencing software, which proved to be helpful and effective.

I traveled to and from Zimbabwe, where I lived with one of my great-uncles whose computers had internet access I would use to complete assignments, tests, quizzes, and discussion boards.

My father passed away in June 1999, and I had to spend some of my savings on funeral expenses, credit card bills, electricity, and telephone bills. I went to live with my great-uncle, who helped me to foot the internet bill expense that was in Harare, and he was more than ready to help me study for my final stage of the ACCA technician exam. But his younger brother recommended that I be careful about his wife, who resented the idea of me staying with them. I lived with them for about four months until one day he got into a domestic dispute his wife. I managed to leave the house, rush to the airport, and go back home to stay with my mother.

I completed my ACCA technician final examinations and went to Botswana to stay with my cousin, who had been residing there for seven years. My goal was to explore employment opportunities that were available to accounting technicians. My cousin and I discussed the trauma that I had gone through as a result of my father's passing and the fact that accounting technicians from other countries would be competing with those locally based on their job history. I stayed in Gaborone for some time and then returned to Lusaka. Having been promised that the ACCA was the leading globally recognized credential allowing one to hold any position in the financial world, I started studying with one of the three hundred approved learning providers. I used DVDs, cassette tapes, videos, and manuals.

But soon I lamentably fell sick. I had a persistent headache. I went to see a doctor who was chief medical officer with the United Nations. She did the bloodwork and diagnosed me with malaria. I could not believe that because I did not have the symptoms that a traditional malaria patient would normally exhibit. The rest of my body was fine except for the headache. I took some painkillers and then took the strongest painkillers, but all that was useless. A friend suggested that I had to see an optician whose prognosis was repetitive eyestrain, and that was what had triggered the headache. He prescribed spectacles. I told my mum that I could see more clearly without glasses. As a result, I chose to get a second opinion from another eye doctor, who after carrying out tests concluded that I did not need the glasses at all. I returned to the doctor who had prescribed the glasses, and he asked me to see a general physician. I did that, and they concluded that I had nothing but depression.

I went to the university teaching hospital and saw a psychiatrist who prescribed Ativan, yet nothing changed. My mother took me to a Chinese hospital, where I underwent a procedure called acupuncture that was supposed to cure me of the persistent headache. It didn't.

My new neighbor, Simon, a devout Christian I had come to know, really got me motivated in the whole area of prayer. He asked me where I thought God was in this situation. We began to talk about the Holy Scriptures like the King James Version of the Bible. Isaiah 53:5 says, "But he was wounded for our transgressions, he was bruised for our iniquities: the chastisement of our peace was upon him; and with his stripes we are healed."

We also looked at the New King James Version. Matthew 8:17 says," He took up our infirmities and bore our diseases." He encouraged me to develop radical faith in God with regard to my situation and told me that it was not his will for me to be sick. He said because Jesus took our physical infirmities and bore our physical pains, he offers us physical healing. Considering another way of looking at my condition, he shared with me the story of Lazarus from the village of Mary and her sister Martha. John 11:21–22 of the New King James Version says, "Lord," Martha said to Jesus, "if you had been here, my brother would not have died. But I know that even now God will give you whatever you ask". His point was I needed an "even now" perspective, for things in this way, no matter how far against the wall I had gone, I was supposed to believe that God could answer our prayers.

At the time, I was doing my ACCA stage 2 exams, which I almost thought I was going to have to defer. I did not. Upon encouragement from my doctor and prayers from my mother, I was able to sit for and pass the exams with flying colors.

I was getting ready to complete my stage 3 of ACCA final exams, but then I started having financial challenges. I called my cousin who was living in Zimbabwe to see if he could help me out, and he agreed to help me find a job. But I was going to have to study and work at the same time. My cousin arranged for me to stay at his farm in Norton. At this point, the persistent headache had gone away on its own without having taken any pill to get up in the morning or pill to go to bed. I got exactly one month off work to study for my ACCA final stage exam.

Prior to this, I had applied for a green card to be allowed to work in the USA. In the summer of 2003, I had just received some correspondence from the US Embassy in Harare that I was to get ready for a series of interviews to allow me to be granted the green card. I needed an address in the US to which the green card would be sent. My brother had a friend who we thought could provide a solution. My great-uncle purchased an air ticket for me through the British Airways. I was going to London in transit to America. I made arrangements with a local pastor in Harare to meet me at the Washington Dulles Airport and then drive to North Carolina, where I was going to work for an accounting firm that was owned by his friend. But that did not work because the pastor let me down. In other words, he did not honor his promise to meet me and pick me up from Washington Dulles Airport. I telephoned my brother's friend, who sent his girlfriend to Philadelphia International Airport to get me.

I stayed with his parents for about a month and then moved to Lancaster, Pennsylvania, to live on my own. Again, all this made me wonder why things were not happening as I had planned. A friend of mine, James, emailed and told me to realize that I was supposed to think about being not the one whole controls life and controls situations and to realize that I was not God after all. This friend quoted Psalm 23:5 of the New International Version of the Bible. "You prepare a table before me in the presence of my enemies".

I had to find a part-time job where people who were on my team were ungodly. I started working for Taco Bell, where I worked for nine months. I worked hard with a team of culinary chefs who collaborated and built on what customers told us they wanted.

After my nine months were up at Taco Bell, I started working at QVC, a company that offered a highly competitive salary plus progressive savings, retirement, and insurance benefits. And speaking of the lifestyle, QVC would stress it was all about the importance of striking and maintaining a proper work-life balance with time off, flexible hours, and other benefits that went above and beyond the basics.

I worked at QVC for another nine months and then moved to working for PFPC. PFPC was a company where one could be proud of integrity and quality of life, which were some of the values that workers demonstrated every day, whether working with peers or listening to clients. All workers embodied and respected an inclusive culture where individuals celebrated unique professional and cultural backgrounds to position the company's serving customer evolving needs. I particularly learned PFPC'S commitment to creating a differentiated experience for its customers driven by a commitment to doing the same for its employees. By focusing on its professional development and providing them with a range of tools to enable them to grow their PFPC careers, they would ensure that they had the right people doing their best work for their customers.

I worked for them for one and a half years. I wanted to work in a mergers and acquisitions role, but they would not let me, so I resigned. Sarah, a Christian I met in Delaware, shared with me from the New International Version, Jeremiah 29:11. "For I know the plans I have for you,declares the Lord, plans to prosper you and not to harm you, plans to give you hope and a future". So I started working as an independent contractor. I worked for different companies through Mass Connections, a company that had advertising contracts with Samsung, Kodak, Walmart, Save-a-Lot, Fresh Grocer, GameStop, Boston Market, and ExxonMobil.

In the end, I was not making a lot of money so I became homeless. I stayed in a shelter called City Team Ministries and then the Salvation Army. Someone tried to steal my car when I was staying at the Salvation Army. One day I went to eat at a restaurant and met a lady called Kimberley. We started talking, and she felt bad for me. She helped me relocate to a better shelter in West Chester. The living circumstances were much better, and I started doing landscaping work in Malvern.

I landed a job with PLCB as a salesclerk. This was through a friend I had met at church: Matt. Matt and I discussed many subjects about our Christian faith. He asked me what kind of job I had intended to do and why. I remember him clearly asking, "Do you want to work on Wall Street like I do? Do you want to make lots of money?" He said, "Money just can't buy everything yet." He asked me to remember King Solomon's experience when he sought what to ask from God. According to 2 Chronicles 1:7 (NIV), "That night God appeared to Solomon and said to him, 'Ask for whatever you want me to give you.'"

And in 2 Chronicles 9–12, King Solomon said, "Now, Lord God, let your promise to my father David be confirmed, for you have made me king over a people who are as numerous as the dust of the earth. Give me wisdom and knowledge, that I may lead this people, for who is able to govern this great people of yours? God said to Solomon,

Since this was in your heart and you have not requested riches or wealth or glory or the life of your enemies—since you have not even requested long life but have asked for wisdom and knowledge to govern My people over whom I have made you king, therefore, wisdom and knowledge will be given you. And I will also give you wealth, possessions and honor, such as no king who was before you ever had and none after you will have".

Another Christian friend, Bob, who was in the meetings that we had with Matt encouraged us to comprehend the dignity of King Solomon's request to the Lord and the things that we should long for as his children. He further reiterated that if anything was worth doing (workwise), it was worth doing well. He also stated why Luke 16:10 (NIV) said, "Whoever can be trusted with very little can also be trusted with much."

Luke16:12 (NIV) says, "And if you have not been trustworthy with someone else's property, who will give you property of your own? But if you are dishonest in little things, you won't be honest with greater."

At the same meeting, another Christian friend, Karen, shared Jesus's parable of the bags of gold. Matthew 25:20–21 (NIV) says, The man who had received five bags of gold brought the other five. 'Master,' he said, 'you entrusted me with five bags of gold. See, I have gained five more.' His master replied, 'Well done, good and faithful servant! You have been faithful with a few things; I will put you in charge of many things. Come and share your master's happiness!'

I moved from West Chester to South Philadelphia, and I started staying in another shelter.

In 2013 I moved to North Philadelphia. Even though I lived in a homeless shelter, I worked and earned almost nothing. I advertised for a pharmacy called E-glam by using my digital, social media, mobile, and email marketing skills. In that experience, my driver's license and valuables were stolen. I moved to central Pennsylvania but was living in a shelter called Sunday Breakfast. There I met a man who was in charge of the residence, and he demanded that I give him money, something that was totally inappropriate, or I had to leave.

Assuming all my options had been exhausted, I decided to start staying outside. I was involuntarily committed to several hospitals during this time and was diagnosed with depression, PTSD, and schizo-affective disorder. After being discharged from the hospital, I lived at a boarding home in North Philadelphia, where I volunteered, helping homeless youth find a place to stay. And that was before I fell terribly sick again.

I moved to Germantown, Philadelphia, in 2015. I met a new friend, Preston, with whom I talked about baseball, and Handy, with whom I went to the local church prayer services. I read the Bible with Handy. We discussed the story of Joseph, the son of Jacob. Even though it wasn't the first time we both learned anything from it, Handy talked about how important it was to be a diligent worker. (When Joseph was taken to Egypt as a slave, he worked hard in Potiphar's house.) He also enunciated the fact that we needed to run from sin at any price. We talked about Potiphar's wife, who became obsessed with and attempted to seduce Joseph, but he left his coat in her hand and ran out of the house. I said to Handy, "Like Joseph, we are supposed to forgive. It was not painless for Joseph to forgive the terrible things his brothers or Potiphar's wife did to him." Even when Joseph had the prospect to take revenge on the people who mistreated him, as an administrator of Egypt, he chose compassion over hatred.

The punitive truth of life can every now and then knock us down, but the life of Joseph proves God's capacity to convert underserved difficulties into a positive outcome. God is in control even when one thinks one's world is out of control. While living in Germantown, I got an opportunity to work in a volunteer position for United Peers, where I helped individuals with intellectual disabilities. That led me to getting a full-time position with Team Arrive, which lasted for nine months. During my time there, I met Haney, with whom I shared my views about chastity. He is the one who introduced the subject. He asked me what my views were, and I explained as much as I could that married people are called to live in matrimonial chastity and others should exercise chastity conscientiously. Those who are promised to tie the knot are called to live in continence. They should see in this time of testing an unearthing of mutual respect, an apprenticeship in faithfulness, and hope of receiving one another from God. They should reserve for marriage the expressions of affection that belong to married love.

He asked me whether there was a relationship between what I told him and the scriptures. Genesis 2:23 (NIV) says, "And the rib that the Lord God had taken from the man he made into a woman and brought her to the man. The man said, "This is now bone of my bones and flesh of my flesh; she shall be called 'woman,' for she was taken out of man."

Genesis 2:24 (English Standard Version) says, "Therefore a man shall leave his father and his mother and hold fast to his wife, and they shall become one flesh." They will help each other grow in chastity, I said.

I also met William during my time at Team Arrive, and with him I discussed the importance of honesty as an attribute. We talked about what it would take to work as a Secret Service agent, and in my and his estimation, integrity was an important trait. He told me that if I ever wanted to work for the Secret Service, he would gladly welcome the opportunity too as a referee for me since that was a requirement. I told him that I particularly thought that everybody is supposed to be honest because truthfulness is the best custom no matter what. Truth and honesty are easier than lying. If you chose to lie, the truth always eventually comes out. Telling the truth is far better than lying, and once trust or reputation is broken because of lying, it can never be completely regained.

I also shared with him that especially in companies and business dealings my personal understanding was that dishonest people will do the job only to make the green and they won't think about the social obligations or others' well-being in this day and age's egotistical world. It may be true that dishonesty can help to make one wealthy, powerful, and famous, but deceitful people can drop from top to bottom in a second. "As you sow, so you shall reap." King Solomon said, Bread gained by deceit is sweet to a man, but afterward his mouth will be full of gravel. Proverbs 20:17 (ESV). William said, "I fully agree."

I moved to Tulpehocken Avenue with Preston while Handy remained on Germantown Avenue. We stayed there for a little while until I moved to West Philadelphia. While living at my newfound apartment, I had no job or prospects and was not feeling too well. I couldn't find anything to do with my time other than go to the Catholic church, which had mass every day. Sometimes I would go to the Lutheran Church, which had church services when the other churches didn't have any. I went to Rittenhouse Park to listen to some musicians play instruments and met Christian students who were distributing food to the disadvantaged. With them we discussed why it was important to eat a healthy and balanced diet. At the park, I educated people why it was not safe for children or adults to play in the fountain as they could contract water-borne diseases from immune-compromised persons. They were people from anywhere playing in the water. Other students I met had faith in God that was deep-rooted, and with them we sang hymns and choruses—some in English, Russian, and German. We talked about Bible stories, such as the chronicles of Noah, King Nebuchadnezzar, Samson, King David, Solomon, Ahab, and Moses.

I had stopped taking my medication because I was thinking that I had started feeling better and no longer needed it. I fell sick again. Thank goodness emergency services had me committed for the second time to a Pennsylvania hospital. I was placed in intensive care for three and a half months and then was discharged because my condition had improved.

When I came home, I wanted to do something positive with my time. My fellow church members at one of the two churches I had started going to, closer to where I lived, advised me to enroll for an American advanced degree in economics. That alone would increase employment opportunities. I looked around for schools and found a place at Lincoln University, where I was accepted to study for the finance MBA. The program was rigorous, and during the midterm of the program, I thought I wasn't going to finish. Perhaps I would have been better off in the human resources concentration. The assistant to the director of admissions advised me that I was, as a matter of fact, better off continuing as a finance major because at that point it wasn't worthwhile to switch specialties.

I followed their lead. I studied hard and sought extra tutorial support and prayers from my fellow believers. I graduated on August 15, 2020, while carrying a straight A average.

I am currently receiving outpatient treatment services from Community Council Health Systems and the Consortium. Since graduation, I have enrolled in a return to the workforce program called the ticket to work program that's managed by the Social Security Administration to help Americans who have disabilities.

Printed in the United States
By Bookmasters